So you think you know Scotland?

So you think you know Scotland?

Adrian Searle
with illustrations by Judith Hastie

**FREIGHT
BOOKS**

Published in the UK 2015

Freight Books
49-53 Virginia Street
Glasgow, G1 1TS
www.freightbooks.co.uk

A CIP catalogue reference for this book is available from the
British Library

ISBN 978-1-908754-89-9
eISBN 978-1-908754-90-5

Printed and bound by Bell and Bain, Glasgow

For Nicola

Introduction

Scotland has always done well in exporting its history and culture, from the arrival of King James IV and I at the English Court in 1603 and Queen Victoria's love affair with the Highlands to Sir Harry Lauder's 'professional Scotsman' Edwardian music hall act to modern day international Scottish icons like actors Ewan McGregor, Kelly Macdonald, and Gerard Butler, musician Calvin Harris, Groundskeeper Willie from The Simpsons and even First Minister Nicola Sturgeon.

Whisky, the kilt and tartan are worldwide brand icons. Films like *Highlander*, *Braveheart* and *Brave* have done today what Sir Walter Scott's romantic *Waverley* novels achieved in the 19th century, taking Scotland to a global audience.

But, as the saying goes, familiarity can breed contempt. When one particular image of Scotland is projected so successfully both inside and abroad, assumptions can be made as to what being Scottish means and who the Scots are.

I hope this book, through its light-hearted scrutiny of surprising, fascinating and sometimes even shocking facts about Scotland, helps challenge some of the obvious, easy stereotypes – while raising a smile at the same time.

I owe a huge debt of thanks to my regular collaborator, the hugely talented artist Judith Hastie, who has contributed some beautiful and hilarious illustrations, greatly exceeding our expectations once again.

Adrian Searle

The shortest scheduled flight in the world is one-and-a-half miles long from Westray to Papa Westray in the Orkney Islands. The journey takes 1 minute 14 seconds to complete.

The official national animal of Scotland is the unicorn.

**Sullom Voe Terminal in the
Shetland Islands is Europe's
largest oil and liquefied
gas terminal.**

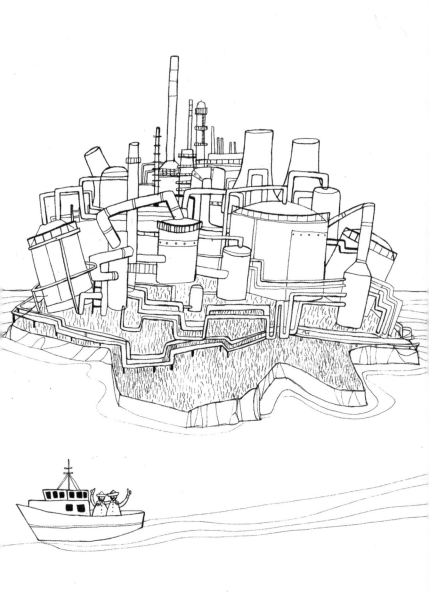

The Bank of Scotland, founded in 1695, is the oldest surviving bank in the UK. It was also the first bank in Europe to print its own banknotes.

The Edinburgh International Book Festival is the world's largest literary festival with over 800 separate events over three weeks in August each year.

Morris dancing was just as popular in Scotland as it was in England from the 15th to the 17th century until it was banned by the Church of Scotland.

The French guillotine was inspired by the 'Aberdeen Maiden', still displayed today in The Old Tolbooth, Aberdeen, a 17th-century former jail that held public executions until 1858.

Scotland was the first country in the world to introduce universal public education for children, passed by Act of Parliament in the early 17th century.

Keith, in Banffshire, is home to the Keith Kilt School, the only school in the world that teaches the art of kiltmaking.

Mount Stuart, family seat of the Marqueses of Bute, on the Isle of Bute, contains the world's first indoor heated swimming pool.

Scotland is home to the oldest tree in Europe, a twisted yew which has stood in Fortingall Forest in Highland Perthshire for 3,000 years.

Scotland has 530 registered golf courses, more per capita than any other country in the world.

The modern bicycle, with a rear wheel driven by pedals, was invented in 1839 in Keir, Dumfriesshire, by local blacksmith Kirkpatrick Macmillan. In 1842 he was fined for knocking over a pedestrian in Glasgow.

Edinburgh has more listed buildings than anywhere in the world.

The Gulf of Corryvreckan, in the Inner Hebrides, has the third largest whirlpool in the world.

There's a memorial to John Lennon in Durness, Sutherland, the only permanent memorial to the former Beatle in Scotland. Lennon spent holidays there as a child between the ages of 9 and 16.

The Edinburgh Festival Fringe is the world's largest arts festival, spanning 25 days and totalling over 2,500 international shows from 60 nations in 258 venues.

Aberdeen Harbour Board is Britain's oldest recorded business, founded in 1136.

The head of any dead whale found on the Scottish coast automatically becomes the property of the king, while the tail belongs to the queen.

The Carnegie Club at Skibo Castle is one of the world's most exclusive private clubs. Membership costs £20,000 per annum.

Scots give more money to charity per capita than any other part of the UK.

Scotland has 790 islands, 130 of which are inhabited.

Dundee is the only city in Scotland that faces south and, as such, claims to be the country's sunniest city.

The longest echo of any building in Britain can be heard in Hamilton, South Lanarkshire, inside the mausoleum of the Dukes of Hamilton. It lasts 15 seconds.

The world's only commercially produced hand-woven tweed is made on the Isle of Harris in the Outer Hebrides.

Scotland is the only country in Europe where Coca Cola is not the best-selling soft drink. In Scotland it is Irn Bru.

The most northerly palm trees in the world are to be found in a private garden near the road between Kirkwall and Stromness, Orkney.

Edinburgh was the first city in the world with its own fire brigade, founded in 1824.

The best place in Britain to see dolphins is Chanonry Point on the Black Isle. It's the location of the world's most northerly bottlenose dolphin population.

Walt Disney is believed to have based his iconic magic castle on Craigievar Castle, Aberdeenshire.

Prestwick Airport is the only guaranteed fog-free airport in Britain.

11 percent of all Nobel prizes have been awarded to Scotsmen.

Fraserburgh in Aberdeenshire is the largest shellfish port in Europe, landing over 12,000 tonnes per annum.

The last British monarch to be born in Scotland was Charles I, who was born in Dunfermline, Fife, in November 1600.

It is against the law to buy or sell cigarettes or any tobacco product in the City Of Glasgow between the hours of 6pm and 6am. This dates back to an 18th century bylaw when Glasgow was the centre of the world's tobacco trade.

Scotland has five universities in the global top 200, the highest number per capita in the world.

N
E
S
North Sea
Highland
whisky
SCOTLAND
Aberdeen
Dundee
St Andrews
Glasgow
Edinburgh

Scotland exported £3.95bn of whisky in 2014. Whisky sales contributed around £1bn in taxes to the UK Exchequer.

The Catholic Church in Scotland has more observed saints days than anywhere else in the world.

St Andrews is home to the world's oldest and most famous 18-hole golf course, the Old Course. The first game is believed to have been played around 1574.

Scots emigres to the USA are five times more likely to become dollar millionaires than those from any other country.

In 1825 John Moir of Aberdeen produced the world's first canned salmon.

Established in 1908, RAF Leuchars, near St Andrews in Fife, was the oldest continuously operating military air base in the world until it was transferred to the British Army in 2015.

**Henry Duncan founded
the world's first commercial
savings bank at Ruthwell,
near Dumfries, in 1810.**

Scotland has the highest proportion of redheads in the world. Around 13 per cent of the population has red hair, with 40 per cent carrying the recessive gene.

The world's first infant school was opened by industrialist Robert Owen in New Lanark in 1816.

A Scotland versus England game at Hampden Park, Glasgow, in 1937 holds the all-time record attendance for an international football match in Europe with 149,415 spectators present.

Over the course of World War One Scotland lost more soldiers per head of population than any other country in the world.

The world's first international football match, Scotland v England, took place on 30 November 1872 at the West of Scotland Cricket Ground, Hamilton Crescent, Glasgow.

HMNB Clyde on the west coast of Scotland, which includes HMS Faslane and RNAD Coulport, is the largest military nuclear base in Western Europe.

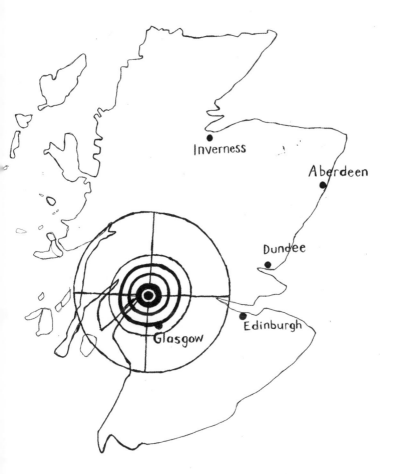

BOMB HERE

The Kagyu Samyé Ling monastery near Langholm, Dumfries and Galloway, is home to the largest Buddhist temple in Western Europe.

Millport, the only town on the island of Great Cumbrae, is home to the smallest cathedral in Britain, and the second smallest in Europe: the nave measures 40ft by 20ft

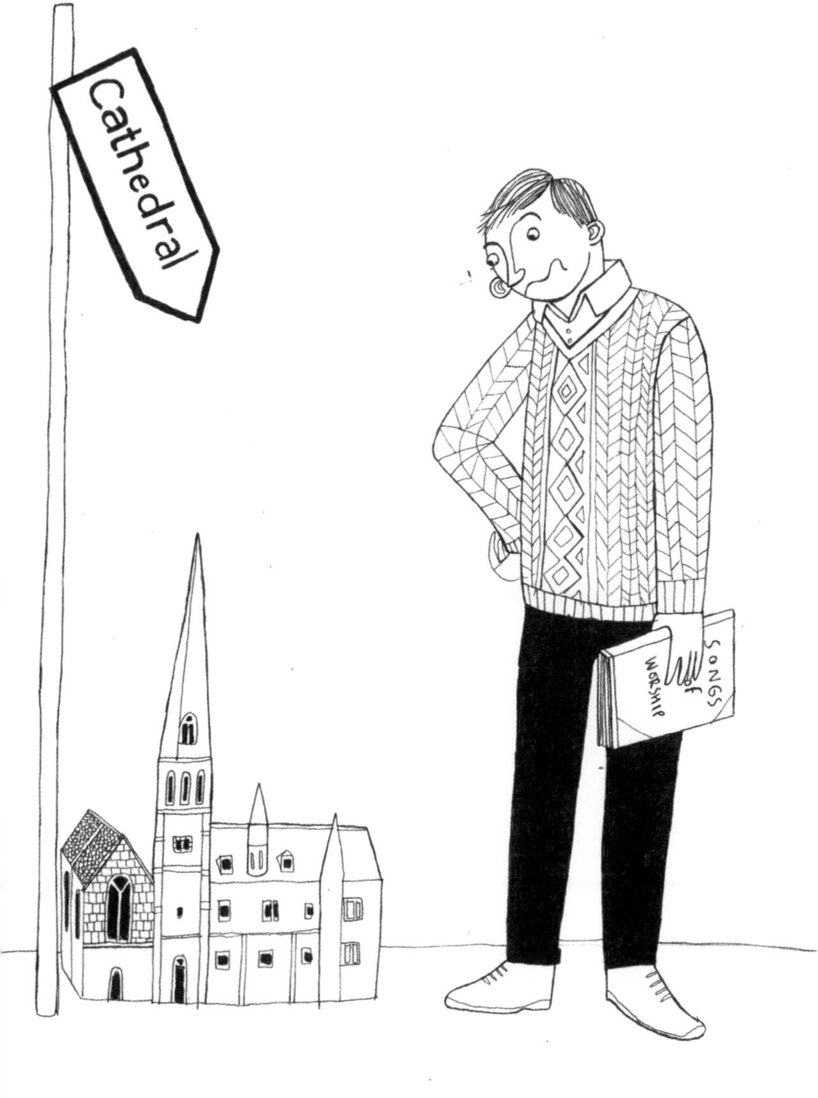
Cathedral
SONGS of WORSHIP

The last person to be accused of witchcraft in the UK was an Edinburgh woman, Helen Duncan, who was convicted of being a witch at the Old Bailey in London in 1944 under an Act dating back to 1735.

In Scotland, it is illegal for a boy under the age of 10 to see a naked mannequin.

Robinson Crusoe, the classic novel by Daniel Defoe first published in 1719, was based on the real experiences of Scottish sailor Alexander Selkirk. Selkirk was left marooned on a South Pacific island in September 1704, surviving there alone for four years before being rescued.

In the Shetlands, between Tingwall and Scalloway, is the 'Murder Stone'. Murderers were chased by their victim's relatives and if they reached the stone alive, they were allowed to live.

START

Haggis, Scotland's national dish, was invented in classical Greece 2,500 years ago.